Wake Up; It's Time to Go to Life

The anti-self-help book for moms

Jessica D. Bowers

TO HANNAH,
MY BIGGEST FAN

Dear Mom:

This book isn't about profound advice. Sometimes the best help you can receive is to know you're not alone. Rip out every page that doesn't resonate with you and keep the rest. From one hopeful human to another, this book will reassure you that one day, we will get it right. Until then, let's take it easy on ourselves.

Belief System:

- PTO days are holy days and are not to be squandered.
- Being present is productive but also painful.
- Lists are counterproductive, an evil force to be reckoned with. While acceptable, grocery and to-do lists are gateway lists and slippery slopes to a full-blown "listorder."
- Soul purpose, not sole purpose; we don't have just one, and overall, it should be innate and not pressured or compared.
- Parenting. You will spend a lifetime trying to process this event. For me, it comes out on paper.

CONTENTS

FOREWORD

I've read a lot of books for moms. *Wake Up; It's Time to Go to Life* was the first one I read where I instantly wanted to be friends with the author. Jessica's writing somehow lays plain the beautiful and scary parts of motherhood in a way that strengthens the reader. It makes you say, "Oh. I'm not alone. I feel ready to do life today." There were paragraphs that put a name to feelings I'd experienced as a mom that I'd never said aloud. There was advice that I didn't know I needed but will cherish forever. *Wake Up; It's Time to Go to Life* is the book every mom with a child aged 10 and up needs. Our diaper bags have long been sold on Facebook Marketplace and given to friends, but we face challenges all our own. *Wake Up; It's Time to Go to Life* is the antidote to the seasoned-ish mom parenting fatigue. It's time to get up and be a mom. But you don't have to do it alone.

- Bunmi Laditan

SHARED PERSPECTIVE

IT'S NOT TOO LATE TO BE… WHO YOU ALREADY ARE

Daydreaming really brings out the "if" in life. If I would have been single for a while before getting married…If I didn't have kids…If I only had one kid…If I would have chosen a different career…on and on. I usually end my daydream by telling myself that no matter what could have been, whatever road I detoured from, that in the most cliché way I am where I am meant to be and allow myself to enjoy the real-life scenery until the next exit.

1,000,001

When I start the day with a donut during my diet, I get stuck with the idea that I already failed for the day, so fuck it. A personal trainer would contrarily state that it is better to get back on the wagon. So, when it comes to parenting, I have to tell myself that if there are a million things I could have done differently already, why make it 1,000,001.

PRESENT

Trying to practice being present with your children is like trying to enjoy the only piece of chocolate cake you will ever get to eat.

EVERYDAY EVE

It's exciting to realize that my New Year can begin on any day. There can also be multiple New Year's Days in the same year. It really takes the load off to realize I don't have to wait weeks, months or a whole year to start working on a goal for myself.

ESSENCE

Sometimes it makes me frantic to think that I might forget any of the cutest things they have ever done. I have to remind myself that I don't need to remember or record every little thing in order to capture their essence. When I think of her birthdays, my heart won't explode any less because I forgot to take pictures of her blowing out the candles. My eyes will still water when I recall the cute way he used his words, even if I don't remember which ones. The core of them will still always be a part of me.

SCARY MOVIE

Everyone suffers from depression. It is always with you, lurking in the background like a horror movie scene you try to get out of your head. Sometimes, the curtain of distraction isn't strong enough to keep it at bay. In those times, you have to try harder instead of letting your mind run with it. When met with a lack of empathy, know that people who can't fathom depression have just never lived in your movie.

POINTS OF LIFE

I will tell my children the point of life is to enjoy the days when you don't question the point of life. The elusive "this is what life is all about" moments we all experience and try to mimic with little success. Maybe those are the only point, the points of life. Everything else is just filler.

STAYGROUND

At times, when my kids would ask to go to the playground, I would cringe at the thought of it becoming an all-day event. How would I Mission Impossible my way out of there this time? Sadly, I came to realize it's only that place for a short time. The place you used to beg your child to leave is now where YOU long to stay for eternity.

SURVIVOR

Motherhood is a group of phases that I simultaneously miss but am also grateful to have survived. Confidently walking through the baby clothes section today without a second thought; Tomorrow, the sight of "Goodnight Moon" taking my breath away.

TOO PROUD

Maybe we were so proud of her, she was afraid to be anything else. As if loving them too much had its own implications. How is love supposed to be a delicate balance? When is there a "right" way to be proud of someone. These are the types of questions I never thought I would consider about parenting, but here I am. The only redemption is their willingness to let you keep trying to figure it out.

NANNY 911

There is a video of my son saying his first word and I hate it. I ruined it but didn't even realize until after I watched it years later. My daughter was trying to be a part of it and I "shhh'd" her. Oh, the agony of witnessing my behavior as if watching it through a lens of Nanny 911. I can hear the narrator in my head "dismissing the daughter in that moment is what will lead to a lifelong resentment towards her mother." Luckily that is not what ended up happening, but to recognize the hurt I could have caused her, might be used as a positive thing. Maybe I can make it up to her by acknowledging it now? She will probably shrug it off or find my apology cringey, but I can try, as I owe it to her.

LIFE (noun):
one or more aspects of the process of living

Emphasis on the "more." I don't want to spend my whole life trying to get my life right. It would be nice to experience the part that comes after.

EARLY BIRD

Being earlier will prevent many regrets. Most of my worst parenting moments were due to poor time management: dismissing my kids' stories when I put them to bed too late, yelling at them before they started the day because we woke up too late, and being stressed when I picked them up from daycare because I didn't leave in time to beat the traffic. If I would have left myself some time, I could have spared myself some regret.

DROUGHT

Seeing your child through a traumatic experience, whether mentally or physically, automatically becomes a traumatic experience for you as well. Like a farmer and his crops in a drought, although you are the secondhand survivor, you will still not be secure after the rain finally comes. The only good thing about the drought it that is makes you notice the clouds.

DON'T FORCE ENLIGHTENMENT

There are days when I have tons of ideas for things to do with my kids, and it all comes so naturally. These don't occur often, so I try to enjoy them when they do. I never expect or aim for this every day. Instead, I accept dull days that aren't destined to be more than that. I think of them like 72 degree weather that I can't will into existence and add them to my mental backlog of "things to look forward to."

MID-LIFE CRISIS

Middle School is the "scary age" of parenting.

KEEP THE DAMN SEASHELLS

For people who find it hard to let go of control, one example I found myself in was at the beach. My kids wanted to collect seashells, and I kept thinking of the piles we already had at home, buckets cluttering our garage. I told them, "No, we don't need them," and I still think about that sometimes. I could have at least waited to get rid of them the following week. They would have been likely forgotten by that time. I won't ruin the next moment, if given one.

GRADUATION DAY

This is the day when I wonder if they will remember to swim parallel to the shore.

NO RAIN, NO FLOWERS: THE POWER OF NEGATIVE THINKING

We have all heard of the power of positive thinking and its importance to practice, but no one ever tells you about the gift of negative thinking. Sometimes it is the only way to survive parenting. Why would I focus on the 20% of parenting that is perfection? My child snuggled up to me with a runny nose while watching our favorite Christmas movie; this is just too painful.

It's better to focus on the other 80% when they are screaming at the top of their lungs the whole day while I have cramps and want to lie down for five minutes. Or, when I have spent hours trying to get them to bed in hopes of spending the last few minutes of the day with your husband, who already gave up and went to bed.

However, it is important to remember to keep your negativity grounded. Don't think about how the runny nose phase will disappear alongside the 2-hour bedtime phase. Or too far ahead when your kid not only sleeps alone but out-of-the-house alone. Your house being quiet all the time is terrifying, even though there are not enough PTO days in the world right now. Why is life like this? "No rain, no flowers." You have to embrace the negative for the positive to exist.

MENTAL LOAD EXPLAINED

We always hear about the mental load that mothers carry. For me, it can be related to the internal gasp of thinking I left the car seat on the top of the car. This occurs randomly and repeatedly throughout the day. Each gasp, while trying to determine if the trigger is truly detrimental, we are interrupted by a thought of the (forbidden) forgotten school snack.

WRINKLE IN TIME

I don't find myself pitying aging characters in television shows. However, I am still surprised every time something inevitable happens to me - a wrinkle, a pain, a vision change - as if it is so tragic or unexpected. How can we better mentally prepare for these milestones so that we are only as intrigued by them as the growing grass?

WAKE-UP CALL

Adjusting to parenthood is like when the sleep just settles in, being jolted by the alarm clock with the realization that they are leaving soon.

MAKE LIFE (MOSTLY) ABOUT THE KIDS

When I am in the thick of it, I need to recall how fast time passes. My toddler became a teenager before I knew it, and that teenager will be out of the house just as fast.

Like most, I became a mom before having the chance to soul-search. Still, I must try to set that aside until after they are out of the house. If I focus only on doing the things that I want while raising kids, I will be filled with regret and a lifetime ahead to do all the soul-searching I wish. Now is not the time to be selfish. My primary focus now is to raise a decent human being before sending them out into the world. I owe that to them—and the world.

PHASED APPROACH

It's hard for me not to think about the phases of my life that are over. The mid-life crisis is real to me now that some of the big milestones are in the rearview and it feels downhill from here. However:

- I am younger today than I will ever be again.
- I have more phases ahead of me worth looking forward to.
- There is always someone in the same phase I am in right now.

ROAD TRIP

Being an overthinker/overprocessor feels like you need to go on a long drive or road trip just to clear your mind, every single day.

CURRENT VERSION

Motherhood is longing for your child in the current moment, not their younger versions (I have forgotten those already). I am realistic now about it happening again, so I mourn them a little each day.

EX

Dwelling on the fact that I am aging feels a lot like listening to friends who are hanging on to ex-boyfriends. It is easy to observe that no one wants to be the person who wastes all their time on something that will never change, so why not look at aging the same way?

SEASONS

In most places, you get to experience at least two changes in seasons in a year; coming out of the coldness or starting to feel its crisp relief. We not only expect this but look forward to it. I don't know of one person that can resist basking in the splendor of these days. They can also occur figuratively. Just when you think the bitterness of your winter is here to stay, you can experience something profound and refreshing. For this, I enjoy reminding myself that a change of season is always right around the corner.

WHY I STOPPED LOOKING FOR CRAP PILES

The best analogy for not worrying came from a therapy session. "If you are constantly looking down for crap piles, you will miss everything around you." Most advice around worrying is that it won't prevent anything from happening. In the case of looking for piles, I guess it might. However, instead of worrying if there was a pile, I shifted to worrying about if there wasn't. I didn't want to miss out on something good for no reason, and in the worst-case scenario, if there were one, I should resolve to handle it and move on.

For example, I worry a lot about my husband and I fading apart and how things will be when the kids leave the house. Staying in that train of thought and mood will most likely cause the exact thing I am worrying about. Why not just focus my energy building our connection?

THE SPACE BETWEEN

Did you know, like most other conditions, empty nest syndrome by definition is more common in women? I am already suffering from it. Pre-empty nest syndrome, PNS? (Reference Page 86) It seems so silly sometimes, since they are still under my roof. I have to equate it to other things to change my perspective. For example, if all I do is sit around missing the "good ole days" once they are gone, it would be no different than if I had spent my entire adult life missing high school. I rarely reminisce that, not just because I hated high school, but more so, I was distracted with my new career of parenthood. I can give myself peace knowing that my life will evolve naturally. The relationship with my kids will just be different when they leave, similar to the times they evolved while still living at home. It also won't hurt to make sure I find something distracting lined up for this era also. Similar concept to retirement I suppose, even though you never retire from parenthood, I will need to keep busy.

So, when they are gone and I am missing them, I will reflect on the not-so-good things to ease the loneliness. I will try to look forward to my empty nest the same way I anticipate the first day of school after a long "I'm bored" summer. I vow to find peace somewhere between the present and future, knowing I will long for both.

UNREQUITED LOVE

I never experienced such intense feelings of betrayal, jealousy, pining, and heartbreak until I had a teenage daughter.

Let me explain. Valentine's Day. The day for love. Typically reserved for couples. However, marketed for all. Flowers for wives, mothers, and daughters alike. I unexpectedly had the perfect Valentine's Day one year with my daughter. I also, unexpectedly, had my heart broken. We drove around delivering treats to her friends. We even stopped at the store beforehand to pick up flowers, some for me (how sweet) and some for a "friend." We had the best conversations, she let me in her world for a while. Later that day, she shared a note from one of her friends, forgetting that it mentioned a secret boyfriend. I was crushed. How could we spend the whole day together with this topic left untouched? I also found out that the second bouquet of flowers was given to another friend's mother. Burned again. There was nothing special about my flowers. Was I being fooled the entire holiday? I have never cried on Valentine's Day and felt so silly for doing so in this moment. We talked and laughed it out and my daughter reassured me that I was being a bit overly sensitive. However, one lesson was learned that day, which is to know your worth in all of your relationships, including the ones with your kids.

WISDOM

Having kids is an exciting time: fresh slate, ignorance is bliss and tunnel vision of being the perfect parent. Everyone gets caught up in this and forgets to flash their headlights for you.

They all tell you to be mindful of how fast time goes by but not of yourself. You have never known yourself as a parent, you don't know how you will react.

No one tells you that you are entering a marathon with zero training. You have never had to have patience like this before.

So, I wish someone would have told me this:

- To notice the first time I didn't like myself as a parent
- To let it scare me
- To treat it like it is my rock bottom, the hangover from hell, the piece of pizza before the heart attack
- Not to shrug it off
- Not to waste my second chance or any chance given subsequently

Even having this wisdom now, I still have to keep my patience in check often. It is a skill that you will be honing the remainder of your parenting career.

RAINCHECK

I have learned to identify when it might not be a good day for the park. When I feel resentful towards my kids, it is not in my best interest to push the limits. When I spend the first half of the day doing things only for them with little or no reciprocation, there is no hope of salvaging any self-esteem. I will simply make a placeholder on the calendar the following weekend for a redo and call it a day.

TIME TRAVEL

Of course, it is taught ad nauseam that every day is a gift and to enjoy it to the (mind)fullest! One tool I use for this is starting the day by imagining that I time-traveled back to it. If the day had been returned to me to restart (from any point in time), its value is priceless. The stakes of making it count are that much higher.

It also makes me laugh to imagine my family reading this section and wondering if I ever do that, because they can't tell.

Either way, it is a nice thought to TRY and hold onto as long as my patience allows. Maybe once, I will live the most perfect specimen of a day.

REGRETS

When my regrets are too much to bear some days, I try to counteract them with fresh attempts. Unlike efforts for health-related goals that are not instant and can be easily reversed, an attempt to connect time with my child will always be well spent.

ICE CREAM DATE

The same magic I can create by surprising my children with a spontaneous trip for ice cream, can be unlocked for myself. Or, even more magical on days that I feel underappreciated by them. I will pick up a donut, ice cream, or some other treat on the way to get them from school and enjoy it in the car line, completely uninterrupted. It will disappear by the time they open the car door. Pro tip, never choose puff pastry or the jig will be up.

A QUIET PLACE

I wouldn't use the word busy to describe a mother since there is no other type. However, I would say there are levels of busyness and that we all possess an internal busyness regulator that keeps our mom mind at bay, right below the quiet place. If not kept in check, a few times a year, the errands, chores, and extracurriculars are caught up just long enough for me to venture there. And when this happens, it can be terrifying. I start having flashbacks of things so sweet yet intangible that I am convinced I am heading to meet my maker. My children's faces, morphing throughout the years in a hazy time-lapse. Faint voices and giggling, as if hearing them from the other room. I quickly snap out of it and scatter to add something to my grocery list in order to shake the feeling. I promise never to judge the "hold my beer" moms again, now that I know their secret.

PROMPTS

Most of the activities in this section are not physical but mental. They are prompts that you might want to take time to meditate on more thoroughly rather than simply reading them and moving on to the next page.

BOYFRIEND

I love taking myself back through an old daydream that is now a reality. Pretty sure this is a daydream shared with the entire population, but it is a vivid one for me. The time when I had a curfew. When I was living at home my senior year and was watching a movie at my, then, boyfriend's house. I wanted to stay the night so badly and be able to wake up next to him. Wouldn't It Be Nice by the Beach Boys comes to mind and it makes me happy that it IS nice now.

THE LITTLE THINGS

Making a mental list of your favorite things in life, no matter how small or simple, is a nice break from the monotony of dishes. The smell right after the rain, cats purring, clean sheets, freshly vacuumed carpets, etc. Remind yourself of all the things you enjoy but might get overlooked in the grand scheme of your day.

LOTTERY

Haven't we all imagined revealing the winning number on our lottery ticket? It can prompt feelings of guilt for me to do this while having food to eat and a roof over my head, but let's just say my retirement account is a little lacking. This fantasy also helps me gain some perspective on my priorities. What things would come first if financial limitations were lifted? What hobbies would I spend time on? If anything stands out, perhaps I can work this into my current schedule. For example, if I would donate to ocean cleanup efforts, maybe in the meantime I could try to find a job in a nonprofit for this cause. Strangely, sometimes thinking of the things you can't do sparks an idea for something smaller that you can.

READY TO DIE

This one isn't fun, but it is more for motivation. The song "Live Like You Were Dying", although a bit dramatic, is always effective at getting this train of thought moving. Obviously, I can't live like I were dying because spending my savings on a trip to a tropical island to live out my days would be irresponsible. However, I can think through what I would have to do to get my house in order. I could also list everyone I would want to talk or write to before I go. Are the people who made the list being prioritized over the ones who didn't? Should I be spending less or any time with the ones who didn't? This exercise is continued in the "Ready to Die Part 2" activity on page 66.

FRESH COAT OF PAINT

Not much in life compares to a fresh coat of paint. I like to sit for a few minutes thinking about the newly painted rooms (literal or figurative) throughout my life. The first move into a place of our own, the baby room, home improvement phases, etc. My mind wanders about the rooms yet to be painted. It can be a struggle to keep it positive, but it is important for me to try.

MORNING ROUTINE

I try to start my day the best way for me by telling myself:

- Whatever scenario motivates me, pretend it.

- Whatever thought will keep my priorities at the forefront, think it.

- Whatever version of myself is ideal, envision it.

- Whatever mantra empowers me, speak it.

- Whatever movement or stillness my body needs, give it.

- Whatever plan that won't bring value, cancel it.

- Today holds the same opportunity that I long for in the past, remember it.

FUTURE

According to Scottish writer, Alexander Chalmers, the three keys to happiness are:

1. Someone to love
2. Something to do
3. Something to look forward to

Number three is the focus here. Some of us find our peace looking forward to short-term, reachable things. We are hasty and worry we won't make the long haul or can't bear the wait. Others are perfectly content investing in the big payoff. Visualizing this keeps them going.

I decided it was important to figure out how I look ahead. Then, took some time to contemplate how my partner does. As suspected, we were finding our happiness in different futures. Well, maybe not the end goal, but definitely the journey. This has helped me to be more understanding of how he operates.

IMPOSTER SYNDROME

I understand that parenthood is a job for which I was utterly unqualified. It is one big learning curve. Similar to life, even if it is halfway through before achieving competence, it is better late than never. I like to take time to draft my own performance review.

I come up with some core values or goals, and then rate myself on whether I meet/exceed expectations and highlight areas for improvement. I can set a yearly reminder on my calendar to go over it. I might leave it as a self-review or get input from my family. Even take it a step further and add some incentives or bonus compensation for myself if I contributed to the overall success of the ~~company~~ family.

IF THE SHOE DOESN'T FIT

I have definitely given up on the idea of wearing certain items because they are restrictive or unflattering. High heels, strapless bathing suits, underwires - It feels nice knowing I never have to think about those decisions again.

I am trying to adopt this same resolve for goals, personas, etc., that don't suit me anymore or maybe never did. To feel confident about the things that just aren't for me. It's not "giving up" to keep wearing uncomfortable shoes, right? So, why do I feel this way in other areas of life? I need to do what works and truly suits me.

There is a personality test called "The McQuaig Word Survey" that I took with one company during my career. As defined on their website, it "measures core personality traits as well as how a person is behaving in their current job." The traits on the results are reflected as "Situational" vs. "Real" and clearly indicate where a person is stretching or performing outside of their authentic self, revealing potential burnout. So, while many motivational books or speakers might recommend going outside your comfort zone, I know that this does not apply to every scenario. Each time I have a big decision to make, I will figure out which outcome will be the 3-inch heels and the other, my flip-flops.

BED REST

I stopped drinking and smoking when I was pregnant. I was also able to truly relax. It was the best excuse I could never make for myself.

Every once in a while, I will give myself permission to rest and take care of myself the same way I did when I was pregnant. Imagining it is essential to my survival. The guilt washes away, while the laundry does not.

GRAND GESTURE

Sometimes, we are so blind to the camouflaged romance in our own lives. It is hidden in them leaving the last clean towel or texting me about an app I might like. When I realized I set the romance bar too high such as waiting on a surprise trip to Hawaii, I turned to the concept of a "gesture jar." Something only I know about, like a special piggy bank or vase with rocks. Every time I notice a small act of intimacy that shows I am still on their mind, I will add an item to the jar. It can't hurt to imagine they have a jar of their own so I should try to do things every day to fill it.

VISUALIZATION

I can sometimes get lost imagining what the days would look like if I had my shit together.

PUPPY ANALOGY

I have used this many times, and it always works. When I struggle with the thought of my kids growing up, I think of a puppy. Most of us don't usually get depressed every day thinking about our dog getting older. There isn't such an emphasis on their age. They don't have as many milestones reminding us of the time passing, and there is no impending doom of them leaving the nest. We merely enjoy their company for as long as they have them. The simplicity of this concept can be very refreshing.

REWARD CHART

The reward/incentive system used for my kids also motivates good behavior for myself. I once lost twenty pounds in a six-week challenge (mostly baby and water weight), because there was $500 on the line. I was never motivated to do something like that before and haven't been again after gaining it back. The brain's reward center is powerful. It's funny that losing the twenty pounds isn't enough of a reward. I try to use this method whenever I need a little boost. When there is a mountain of laundry, I work out a trade with myself. "Whether a cinnamon roll or a sugar-free caramel latte, it can all be yours (after you do your chores)."

MY LIFE AS A SONG

I like to sit and think about a favorite song.

How does it sound when:

- Muffled by the wind when the car windows are all down

- Out on the water

- Remixed

- Sipping red wine

- Quiet, in the background of a conversation

- After a long day or a big decision looming

- Raindrops are hitting the roof

- Irrelevant or ironically relatable

- Brand new, overplayed, or forgotten

- It has a new meaning, or you hear a lyric you never caught before

When it feels like my life in most cases won't change, I can still find new ways to experience it.

REDEFINE YOUR GOALS

Generic goals sometimes get lost, such as "lose weight," "have a good relationship," etc. In my case, one of them is for my daughter to want to spend time with me once she leaves home. One day, during a good phase, I noticed she put a picture of us on her bookshelf. After that, I started to remind myself of a goal to "stay on the shelf." This became more achievable than simply trying to maintain the good phase. I try to tie a specific feeling/memory to my goals to make them more attainable.

BUCKET LIST:

1. ~~Stop making lists~~

As mentioned at the beginning of this book, if this section does not apply to you, skip or rip out this page.

Lists have been holding me back my whole life. I have a dear friend with whom I have commiserated often about this, and I also watch my dad suffer from his "listorder."

If there were ever a My Strange Addiction episode about me, it would be lists. Even though nothing feels as liberating as consolidating or eliminating them, I keep making new ones. It is a form of self-sabotage. Like with most other bad habits, the key to stopping is figuring out why one does it. (While this is not the intent of this activity, I might spend some time investigating that separately).

It is a known form of anxiety-related OCD. I feel in control when I have everything on paper, but it is counterproductive. As with other theories about removing clutter and creating space for better things, this is also true regarding lists. I can simply exist when I am not bound to an unachievable checklist.

Of course, there are necessary (temporary) lists for groceries or daily reminders. Anything outside of that, I have to believe that the essential things will get done. For example, there is no point in putting "clean out closet" on a to-do list because it will stay there until I am in the mood to do it anyhow. So, if I have every intention to do chores or take the kids to the park on Saturday, but instead wake up feeling decisive and energized, I should choose to be spontaneous and order the kids pizza and a movie while I handle the closet. The chores can be put off a day.

The stars will likely align for me to "call sister" long before it gets crossed off. It is pointless to keep carrying over items like this, not to mention stressful, to insinuate something is a high priority just because I wrote it down.

Lists are like extra weight – adding things to the list is much easier than removing them. Proceed with caution. The age old Nike slogan, "Just Do It," is helpful for me to keep in mind. It might not always be a convenient time to do something, but the more I practice this habit, the better.

This activity is about acknowledgment at this point and can be followed up with the section about list-making's ugly cousin, Virtual Hoarding, which is up next.

VIRTUAL HOARDER

We always hear of hoarding and picture a house full of newspapers, Taco Bell cup collections, cats, and 20 toothpaste tubes due to extreme couponing. At least, that is what I imagine.

Another type of hoarding most of us do (while having super-organized homes) is virtual hoarding. If you are like me, you might have a Google Drive full of screenshots or texts/emails to yourself of articles you want to remember. To make matters worse, almost every app we use has a Favorite button. It can be quite mentally draining. I realize it is as important to clear my mental cobwebs as the ones above my cabinets.

How were things different before the age of information overload and over-inspiration? I believe these problems still existed, but in a different form. I can imagine people watching Oprah when they got home from work and either recording episodes on VHS or writing down tips and tricks in a journal, such as making a list of books from Oprah's Book Club or keeping notebooks full of cut-out magazine recipes that would get dusty over time.

It is hard to break free of the need to store everything you think you will forget. However, we can take advantage of this era of all information at our fingertips and let go of creating these virtual scrapbooks. I know this is SUPER hard to do, but I start by taking a PTO day (or two), making a temporary list of all the places I store things of this nature, and then performing a virtual detox.

Do I REALLY need to save articles on "How to make your own granola," "Ten things never to put in the dishwasher," or "How to create a cozy patio nook?"

Saving things like this makes me feel complete and unnecessary pressure. If I ever think to myself, "Hmmm, I want to try and make my own granola today," I find comfort in knowing I can Google it.

I also tend to get wrapped up in the "activities to do with your kids" type articles and have to remind myself that I can Google that, too - I can Google all the things!

If I must keep some things, I consolidate them into one app I like the best. I have also created an email folder and send all articles there or use Pinterest to categorize things I want to keep (recipes, haircuts, etc.).

Creating a system of organizing related items in one place is essential. If I have saved parenting articles in digital format, but also physical parenting books on a shelf, I make myself pick one or the other and print out the most essential articles for a notebook on my bookshelf.

Lists can be good for reference purposes, rather than a nagging to-do list. That being said, when I have multiple lists like "things to do with the kids," I use this activity to consolidate them and assign a designated location, so they are no longer a collection of screenshots on my phone.

I just make sure to be in a purging and decisive mindset. Then, I grab my coffee and answer the following questions about each article I come across:
1. Is this something I can google later?
2. What are the chances I will actually go back and read this?
3. How long ago was this article saved, and did it affect me during this whole time I forgot it was even there?
4. If this was on Oprah twenty years ago, could I simply watch it, retain the information if it was important to me, and then move on with my life?

Pretending like I am the therapist called in on my own episode of (virtual) Hoarders feels empowering and tends to do the trick.

ONE PTO DAY AT A TIME

A PTO day is one of the most life-saving gifts. While some people reserve them for appointments or to binge-watch TV in peace, I usually use them to sit and process life, which I guess is also called meditating. I am still determining if I ever learned to meditate correctly, though. I can sit in one place for hours, but instead of having a clear mind, I think deeply about all my trains of thought that get interrupted daily. Embarrassingly, I have even made lists of things to "finish thinking about" on my days off.

When I feel I have too much self-improvement work to prohibit me from thoroughly enjoying a Netflix day, I will use this time to chip away at it. For example, if I recently watched an episode of Marie Kondo's Joy of Tidying Up and want to go through and purge all of my belongings. Or I am completing the Ready to Die Part 2 activity from page 66 of this book and want to take a day (or multiple) to get my house in order.

I also use my PTO for date days! No need to worry about a babysitter. I just have to ration out how many days I want to spend solo vs with my husband. Note: Non-paid days off count too! Even in the times I am not employed full-time, I make sure to set aside a day to focus only on things for myself. I know I have accrued some.

COMPARE YOURSELF TO OTHERS

I know this is a faux pas and would not likely be recommended by one of my motherhood gurus, Kristina Kuzmič, but it is just one of my coping mechanisms. Comparing, whether negatively or positively, helps me gain perspective.

When I picture someone I admire, I think of what I can incorporate in my life to mimic the aspects I find appealing about them. Health conscious, financially disciplined and gentle parents in the wild. What habits should I let go of or incorporate to get closer to a similar version of myself?

On the contrary, thinking about all the pet peeves I have about other people can be very effective in appreciating my good qualities. Sometimes, I will point these out to my husband, "Aren't you so glad I don't…" to which he exclaims, "Yes!" Then, I will think of one for him, saying, "I am so glad you aren't like…" and we always end up laughing.

FIRE DRILL

Similar to how fast I can clean my house when I find out someone is stopping by at the last minute, pretending there is a fire can metaphorically light one for me. When in a purging mood, I imagine my smoke detector going off other than from my frozen pizza. Aside from furniture or clothes, I try to get rid of most other items I would not take in the event of a fire. Old Karate Gi's, gone. Boxes of unused school supplies, donated. Photo books promptly backed up to the cloud. All done just in time for the pizza!

DRIVE-BY

If your current housing situation is in dire straits, skip this. Otherwise, this activity can be done with your kids.

On my most grateful days, I am still guilty of being tempted to want more, bigger and better things. I have driven around fancy neighborhoods in wonder and admiration. In order to balance my gratitude after these trips, I make sure I am in the same mindset before turning back onto my own street. Pulling up and gawking at the beauty of the place I get to call home, that so many others might drive by thinking the same. Remembering the pride I felt at the thought of ownership, before the newness wore off. Even if I am not where I want to be forever, my home is the haven I was looking for at one point in time and is serving that purpose for me now. And after this practice, it always it feels a thousand times cozier.

LIFE IN AGILE

In a past life, I worked in the technology field and learned about a project management system called Agile Methodology which has benefits when applied to my personal life as well.

1. Daily scrum – A quick status check on my goals and to identify any blockers.

2. Refinement – taking time to update any requirements. Making sure not to leave my backlog item of "Meal plan" with just the title. Taking the time to figure out the meal goals and strategy.

3. Estimation – Making sure I don't fit too much into my sprint.

   - 8 hours sleep

   - 8 hours work

   - 8 hours play

4. Retro – Taking time to reflect on what went well and what could be improved. Practicing the exercise of deciding what to Stop/Start/Keep.

5. Scope creep – Saying "no" to unplanned activities to ensure I can accomplish everything that I planned.

READY TO DIE PART 2

After writing this section, I came across an article about Swedish Death Cleaning, which reinforced my own beliefs about the importance of this ritual. Google it for reference if you need further inspiration.

Being ready to die isn't the same as wanting to die. Sure, the initial thought is that if I can die happy now, what is the point? It is to prioritize getting the house in order, so you can truly enjoy the time you have. The thought that my loose ends can be tied before the end gets closer is appealing and I will be able to focus on more meaningful things. Also, not to be morbid, but I know there is always the chance that I might not be fortunate enough to prepare for it.

I keep my bucket list short and as a nice to have—not one that drives me crazy every day that it is not complete. Thinking of it this way: I have lived your life up until now without going to the Maldives, so if it happens, it happens. If not, it's okay. On the other hand, if I start losing sleep about it every night, book the trip and make it happen! The true things I feel compelled to do will become apparent. They are different than just a travel board of things Instagram and other social media apps make me feel I should do.

Looking back at my Parenting Pinterest board, I feel dumb for even adding "50 Rainy Day Crafts." My kids somehow survived without making fake snow, but the pressure to do something special on those days was not lost on me.

So, what are examples of loose ends? These things can vary depending on the priorities of each person. They could be high-level items such as bills and passwords or personal items such as keepsakes and pictures. So, if/when that time comes, I won't worry about whether or not my loved ones can log into my insurance account or come across some cringey love letters long forgotten about.

Taking action: I make a (temporary) list of things to be compartmentalized. I never attempt to start this while the kids are home or plan to get to it a little "here and there." It needs to be very intentional and will probably require some PTO, maybe up to a week. It's totally worth it.

SAMPLE SCHEDULE:
      Monday - Recipes
      Tuesday - Photos
      Wednesday - Sentimental items (see below)
      Thursday - Virtual hoarding detox
      Friday - Important info (gathering all financials and passwords, etc.)

The room-by-room approach can work if dedicating a day or so to each room. Note: I understand some people could care less about if their recipes are organized when they die. It is just an example of something that might have been on someone's to-do list for a long time, or they may have family recipes they want to pass down.

Sentimental items: This is obviously the hardest category, but it helps to ask myself, "What is the point of storing things in a box that sits in a closet?" If I have multiple boxes, I need a challenge to reduce it to only one box. I will need to be creative and pick out favorite drawings/schoolwork and scan them for a physical or virtual photo album. There are a few companies that offer this service.

Alternatively, I may choose to turn some of the items into pieces of décor. This way, they are displayed and can be enjoyed instead of being in storage. For example, I used to document cute quotes my kids would say. I printed some on decorative paper and framed them for a small wall collage in my office. Likewise, I could print them out on a yearly basis and put them in a corresponding photo album, so my memorabilia is in one place. Another puppy analogy incoming. You don't write down things your puppy does or keep all the items they touch; you simply enjoy being with them.

Once I have completed this exercise, I feel like a new person. My focus is restored and there is a sense of not only being ready to die, but even more to really live.

REPURPOSE

Purpose

Noun: The reason for which something is done or created or for which something exists

Verb: Have as one's intention or objective

I used to get extremely hung up trying to figure out my purpose instead of figuring out how to live purposefully. Eventually, I realized my success could be measured by how little I regret. Doing this makes it much easier to define how I want to live.

1. I don't want my marriage to be broken.

2. I don't want my kids to hate me.

3. I don't want to feel like I am destroying my body or health.

4. I don't want to waste time on superficial relationships.

These can all be my purpose. I try to use my bucket list to get out of the day-to-day. Up to this point, I have always waited until things were perfect, or simply where they needed to be, to figure out my purpose. It is as if once my mind is clear, it will just present itself to me after all these years. The thing is that most relationships can't wait until you are ready.

Many people don't change the world in a history book sense. There are hundreds of ways to say that you can change it on a smaller scale through your interactions with those around you.

When I need additional validation, I think about people I admire and want to imitate. Have they won a Nobel Peace Prize or invented a green energy alternative? Or am I drawn to them because they are enjoying their life and seem to have all the answers on how to be happy?

I periodically spend a few minutes deconstructing the notion of my purpose and ensuring a clearer vision of it going forward.

POETRY AND PROSE

1,000 KISSES A DAY

Scared, unsure
While you were inside
Until that very moment, with Daddy right beside
1,000 kisses a day, as soon as we saw you

On the top of your head
The tip of your toes
Ears, cheeks, your precious little nose
1,000 kisses a day, all over you

While you were asleep
Right when you awake
After every bath you take
1,000 kisses a day, the whole day through

41 times an hour
No time for shopping
Working, or a shower
1,000 kisses a day, is all I want to do

To talk or eat
Are what lips are for
Not now, but at least before
1,000 kisses a day, to no one until you

As you age and grow
My affection
You won't let me show
1,000 kisses a day, I'll long to give to you

I will learn to make due, I guess
But until that time
There will be nothing less
1,000 kisses a day, to show my love for you

SECOND

Baby one, my first love
Am I ready for a second?

Counting down, nine months to go
I can't wait to meet my second

Will I have enough love to share?
As for place, there'll be no second

You are here, in my arms
All it took was that split-second.

Watching every breath you take
I don't want to miss a second

I've been here before and learned my lesson
It goes by faster than a second

Would not trade you for the world
So happy that I had a Second

FLEETING STAR

You are my fleeting star
Full of wonder, traveling far

You disappear as I stare
I already miss the smell of your hair

Going so quickly by
All the mysteries I can't answer why

Don't burn out, wish I could catch you in a jar
My little fleeting star, you are

HE

He cries when it's not time to wake up
And then cries once again when it is
He pesters his sister by taking her toys
And telling her that they are his
When the banana breaks in half
He hurls himself down on the floor
He always escapes from the grocery cart
And made me trip over myself at the store
He screams when I butter the wrong side of the toast
But won't eat a bite anyhow
He swings at me when I tell him "No"
And says he wants things "right now!"
He makes such a terrible mess
But hates when I pick up his stuff
He whines when I help him get dressed every day
And don't tie his shoes fast enough

I yell and I scream back at him sometimes
But he loves me the same anyway
He asks me what day it is "no school, no work?"
Longing for Saturday, every day
He tells me to snuggle "one more minute"
And says that he loves me "the best"
We have our own jokes, and hearing him giggle
Always leaves me so powerless

The most inconvenient thing I will ever love
No time left to take care of me
But like a bare oak with its roots in the winter
I can't stand on my own without He

MOTHER
(I promise, in rare occurrences, your daughter will see you as another human)

I can see her take account of me

My dusty jewelry on the stand

I am not allowed to like this song

"Why are you even wearing that brand?"

I can only tell if she wants me near

From her lack of pure disgust

Her initial reaction

Is sometimes all that I can trust

But sometimes she is off her guard

One way or another

She sees me as her counterpart

Not only as a mother

LET'S GO

Your dangling legs, hanging from my waist

Walking through the pet store

Added to the list of things

You don't want to do anymore

AMATEUR

What a fool I was when I would wonder if my life would "always be like this." It didn't take long to realize my life would never be like that again. Longing to:

- Stroll you around the house at 3 a.m. - the sleep doesn't seem to matter as much now.
- Drive endlessly through the neighborhood at nap time - I no longer have better things to do.
- Pick you up from daycare - I would give anything to see your face light up for me once more.

How stupid to count down the time until those phases were over. As clumsy as cleaning out the pantry before a hurricane.

I expected some relief after these milestones. Instead, I was met with another locked chapter I would try to claw my way back into during my saddest daydreams.

PAINFUL MEMORIES

Friday nights, the best nights
Your tiptoeing on the floor
The relief in your eyes
To stay up a little more

You reaching through the seats
When I sat behind you on the flight
It reminded me of Dumbo
Everything would be alright

Singing in the shadow
Of the music in the car
I cheered for you internally
The sweetest little star

The way you rubbed your lips
With your thumb when you were sleepy
To imagine it even now
Is making me feel weepy

You liked the color sepia
But didn't know its name
You knew the way it made you feel
Which made me feel the same

I wish I had amnesia
For dwelling in times like these
Would spare myself the slightest
From these painful memories

PARENTING IS

Dipping your toe in the bath

Taking a sip from the glass

Turning the volume down low

Missing the best part of the show

Waking up early after a long night

Just about to take a bite

Never felt this old

Your coffee always getting cold

About to head out for a bit

"Sorry, I just can't make it"

Weekends spent folding clothes

Paid time off to wipe their nose

Wondering where the time went

Didn't even make a dent

Feel yourself slowly losing the way

Hoping to get back on track the next day

PLAN B

Strive for peace
"You are where you are meant to be"
Let there be one goal
To live angst-free

No matter the diversions
Success, or tragedy
"Life is all about
How you handle Plan B." – Suzy Toronto

WORKING PARENT

Come on, babe, wake up, this is nothing new

Trust me, I don't want to go any more than you do

Hurry up, let's go, it's 6:38

If we leave past 7:00, we're going to be late

I don't think I can make it to the book fair

I'm sorry, but today I just can't be there

Bumper to bumper, all this internal conflict

Is it anxiety, or am I just getting carsick?

I only see you three hours a day

And that's only if nothing else gets in the way

I know I said I would pick you up by 6:00

But I had to stop and get gas really quick

And I am sorry I forgot to sign your school letter

Tomorrow, I will try and do better

Alright, sit down and eat, get up rinse your plate

I know you wanted to play, but it will just have to wait

Yes, it is already time for your bath

But first, can you quickly finish your math

Time for bed, although we just got home it seems

I hope you have lots of sweet American dreams

WAR OF PARENTHOOD

Humbled by just how much
This fight was underrated
Even with all your training
It could never be abated

Post-traumatic battle wounds
And lost identity
Hoping for a safe return
Longing for normalcy

Forever changed, self-sacrifice
And all that was invested
Your worst version on display
Every fiber of you tested

Bravery subdued,
You must surrender to survive
It will be your greatest victory
If you make it out alive

Although not scared of dying
Part of you has before
This wasn't in the contract
But "all is fair in love and war"

DAYS SINCE INCIDENT

Every morning starts the same
Painfully ambitious
First day of the rest of their lives
Try to keep them in your subconscious

Different pages already
How quickly the patience wanes
The tone has been set
But, still, the hope remains

Forgetting my studies, what was that part again
Something about pausing
Keep your voice down low
To subdue the stress you're causing

As the day goes on it's clear
I should surrender, just go back
Retrace every step and see
How things got so off-track

Every night, my thoughts catch up
My ritual of repent
Vowing my tomorrows won't just be
0 days since incident

EMPTY NE(STING)

Just like that, you were here
And just as soon you're leaving
How quickly celebrating
Can turn into grieving

Unable to even recognize
The girl who once was little
This era that felt like a novel
Is now a chapter in the middle

I can't hear you somewhere in the house
And call you to come down
Or feel your presence in the car
While driving around town

Even though not gone for good
I will still miss you in that way
My maternal purpose is off-track
You won't be back to stay

No longer under my sole care
Anxiety re-routed
Hoping you'll adhere to
All the lessons that I touted

I find myself some days
Trying to recall
The lasts of things I did with you
And how I missed them all

The last book we read together
The last time you picked me a flower
Who knew these tiny memories
Could carry so much power

I now envision relevance
And how to make you stay
Wishing for regular visits
Not just on Christmas Day

I hope that in your hindsight
It feels like your favorite song
You know now more than ever
How much I loved you all along

NAP TIME

Oh, if time could be frozen

Like the snow on the trees

I could smell your hair and kiss your chubby hand

For all eternity

ONE THING

If you remember one thing, I hope it is that I was always trying to be better and not that I could have loved you more. If I could go back and do it all over, there is a lot I would have changed, but how much I loved you would always be the same.

GRAPEFRUIT

The day ended how it began, bittersweet, just my breakfast: Coffee, bitter with a pinch of sugar, and my grapefruit, also with a pinch of sugar.

I sat on the patio, wondering how much longer I had to myself.

The day went on, and I longed for the next quiet time. And when I have it, imagine when I will have an eternity to eat my grapefruit.

HALF-PAST NOW

Living in the moment is so painful.
Noticing each moment leave you, closer to tomorrow.

Being mindful of how quickly Sunday passes makes me anxious,
constantly aware the ticking clock.

My goal is to be oblivious of time.
Time makes me yell, makes me bitchy, makes me restless.

I will pretend like I have all the time in the world.
Time to heal and change at my own pace, no pressure.

They say that when you stop trying to solve a problem, a solution
presents itself. So, maybe when I stop paying attention to time, it
will become limitless - a happy home, instead of a productive one.

I need to live in the future, not the present. A future where my kids
come to visit, and my husband and I have hobbies. And I am not
bitter about how I wish I had done things differently.

Maybe I will get a tattoo of a clock—not to remind me of the time
passing but of the future. "Half-past now"

HAPPY MOTHER'S DAY

I didn't see my kids all day.

I didn't hear my daughter say how much she hates her brother and wishes he was never born.

I didn't give up something I had planned to do for myself in order to take them to the park and fight with them about leaving.

I didn't have to listen to them (after the park) say that they were bored and that we never do anything fun.

I didn't make them lunch and hear them say they wanted something else.

I may have spent this Mother's Day reflecting on all my failures as a mom, but at least I did it in silence.

KITE

I am sorry.

I expect so much from you. Perfection - but I know you are just like the kite.

Beautiful and soaring and free when the wind is right.

I don't get mad at the kite, so why would I get mad at you?

NEW YEAR'S 2.0

It's that (second) time of year again. New school year, new me. I actually do a pretty decent job keeping up with book fair dates, school spirit nights, and penny collections throughout the year. However, I am a sucker for a good self-improvement opportunity. Make healthier lunches, make more lunches period. Wake up earlier, less tardies, nightly reading log, etc.

We cleaned out her closet and organized her desk, all of the new-year-type rituals. "This year is going to be different," I think to myself. I have been listening to an audible book on parent-child communication, so that maybe we won't yell every night. I can reverse going down the path of a Maury-like mother/daughter dynamic I have been projecting. Who knows? I may end up back in the same place next year with that same feeling I have when Target puts out the bathing suits, but I at least have to try.

Besides, after last year with a horrible teacher, my daughter told me the other night that 2nd grade wasn't so bad. Maybe she will have even fonder hindsight about her mom, who might not put a note in her lunch box every day, but always did on the first one.

PAINFULLY PRESENT

I look up from my grocery list while in the car rider line and stare at the brick building. The scene imprints in my mind. The clanking of the flag against the pole when the wind blows, the sun shining through my visor. (I got there a few minutes earlier, resulting in the sunny spot of the line). It's a blue sky, crisp air kind of day, and everything is quiet for a few more minutes before the bustling of stir-crazy kids crash through the doors like a scene from The Walking Dead. I feel so sad that I chose to take in this moment instead of hastily waiting for the bell to ring as usual. I know now that this imprint will be so painful to me when we drive by in a few years, and all it will be is a landmark. "Aww, remember when you used to go there," we will say, and then forget about it a few minutes later. My eyes water a little right before you get in the car. I can't imagine when this is no longer a part of my routine. I yearn for it already as you are giggling about your day.

BALANCE

I went to a cupcake store today to buy a birthday treat for a friend. On my way in, I passed a fellow mom. In the blink of an eye, I used my tribal knowledge to fully assess her situation. I felt like a detective, checking off all the telltale signs in my head as I walked by and gave her a half-smile. She was having a day I had had before.

About to come out of a kid's hair salon, she looked unscathed for the most part. Physically, she was not disheveled and seemed to have everything under control. She was not the "type of mom" to have unruly children, or like most of us, wanted others to think she was. There was just one more errand on her list, if she could complete it before pushing the lunchtime envelope.

Once inside the store, the kids were increasingly awful. I felt like I was having an out-of-body experience. All my emotions competed: empathy, pity, anxiety. I even felt some form of resentment towards her, perhaps for triggering my own PTSD. Mostly, what I felt was guilt.

Usually, I would have joked about the terrorist-in-disguise I had left in the car with his tablet, specifically for this reason. I didn't, or would ever, sneer or roll my eyes at this peer of mine. I simply froze for some reason out of my control. Did I enjoy that she might think I was childless and envy me? Was it my sheer morbid curiosity to see the scene play out for someone else? Was I trying to keep quiet to minimize the chaos for her? I will never know.

However, things didn't end when I left the store. The scene lingered with me on my ride home. Like when you accidentally run over an animal, and you have flashbacks of it the whole day, I kept thinking of this mother.

The little boy was whining and rolling around on the floor. She had to chase him from behind the counter and apologize profusely while her little girl ran towards the door, grabbing things off the shelves on her way. The mother was visibly embarrassed that she did not, in fact, have her shit together as she presented. She ended up leaving before purchasing her items, telling the cashier that she would be back after putting the kids in the car.

I kept wondering what happened when she was finally able to escape to the car. Did she lose all sense of herself and start screaming at the kids for embarrassing her? Or was she the type to be able to keep her composure, then cry quietly after she finally got them down for a nap? Maybe her nightmare even continued when she got home.

My thoughts were finally interrupted when I saw the blinker of a car trying to squeeze in front of me to get out of the wrong turning lane. The driver's eyes met mine, pleading. I glanced quickly and saw a rear-facing car seat in the back. A vivid memory was recalled, of my own screaming infant on an endless drive home. I gestured to her nicely and urgently with my hand and a head nod to please go ahead. At that moment, balance was restored in my universe of motherhood.

MORE

I love you more than the cool, crisp air
At the first sign of fall
More than words used to describe
Everything, most and all

I love you more than the tallest mountain
And everything in view
More than coffee in the morning
With cream and sugar, too

I love you more than all the leaves
From every single tree
More than I love anyone
Even more than me

I love you more than all the riches
Than the greediest desire
More than all the embers
Of a raging forest fire

I love you more than all the seconds
That slip away somehow
Starting from the beginning of time
And infinite years from now

I love you more than all the water in the seas
And the sand on every shore
No matter the comparison
I will always love you more

PLANT ME AS A MAPLE TREE

I do not want a funeral
For everyone who is going
To pick a seat to watch your pain
Like a private movie showing

No need to get me an outfit
Or tell them how to do my hair
I don't want you to stand over me
When I am not even there

Don't want you to have to pick
And play my favorite song
Or have a memory of my face
With my makeup done all wrong

I don't want you to plan the day
Get all dressed up to cry
And feel like it's the only time
You have to say goodbye

I don't want people who forgot me
Until they heard the news
To show up and say goodbye to me
And simply pay their dues

The people who really knew me
And cared about me most
Will show up to take care of you
Until it's time to leave their post

(cont.)

Then plant me in the ground
As a maple tree
The roots will start surrounding you
As you're standing next to me

My leaves will swirl all around
Or fall gently on the snow
You'll pick one up occasionally
And take me with you when you go

With each and every season
When the change of colors start
Those perfect shades of reds I loved
Will keep me in your heart

As I continue growing
The stronger we both will be
I do not want a funeral
Plant me as a maple tree

ABOUT THE AUTHOR

Jessica D. Bowers lives with her husband and two children in Waxhaw, NC, outside of the larger Charlotte area, which she has called home since college. In her first book, *Wake Up; It's Time to Go to Life – the anti-self-help book for moms*, she explores the never-ending struggle of balance in parenthood. With her introspective essays and poetry, she manages to explain the common mother experience in a comforting and unique voice.

www.jessicadbowers.com

JESSICABOWERS111

ACKNOWLEDGEMENTS

JD, your unconditional love is all anyone could ask for.

My children, Brynn and Ian, this book would not exist without you. You created a new dimension of emotions for me that I will never fully be able to describe.

Mom and Dad, thank you for your unwavering support in everything I attempt. It is at my core and will always be in my subconscious.

All the people in my life, like Diane, who might think their encouragement was insignificant. It wasn't. It made such an impact and pushed me to keep the idea of this book alive.

Made in USA - Kendallville, IN
36953_9798332392733
12.27.2024 2056